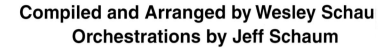

Gold Star Favorites
Primer Level

Compiled and Arranged by Wesley Schaum
Orchestrations by Jeff Schaum

T0081812

Preface

This series offers students an appealing variety of styles in a single album. A brief paragraph of background information is provided for most pieces. Folk music includes spirituals. Jazz styles include boogie, blues, ragtime, swing, and rock.

All books include audio with orchestrated accompaniments. Each piece has two tracks:
1) Performance tempo. 2) Practice tempo. An optional duet accompaniment, based on the orchestration, is included for all pieces at the early levels.

The intent of the audio is to provide an incentive with a demonstration of the finished piece. The slower practice tempo assists the student in maintaining a steady beat, using the correct rhythm and gaining valuable ensemble experience while making practice more fun.

Contents

To access audio visit:
www.halleonard.com/mylibrary

Enter Code
7612-1075-5547-1318

ISBN 978-1-4950-8209-2

Schaum

EXCLUSIVELY DISTRIBUTED BY

HAL•LEONARD®

7777 W. BLUEMOUND RD. P.O. BOX 13819 MILWAUKEE, WI 53213

Visit Hal Leonard Online at
www.halleonard.com

This African-American spiritual has roots in the Bahama Islands in the Caribbean Sea. There is a tradition, going back to the early 1900's, that this spiritual is played at funeral processions in New Orleans, Louisiana. The tempo going to the cemetery is slow. It is played faster when the procession leaves the cemetery.

Duet Accompaniment

Accompaniment notes with stem UP are to be played with the RIGHT hand.
Notes with stem DOWN are to be played with the LEFT hand.

 Track 1: Performance tempo
Track 2: Practice tempo (played twice)
(Each track includes two-measure introduction)

When the Saints Go Marching In

Animato

African-American Spiritual

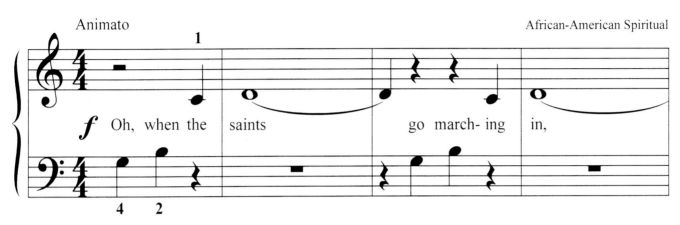

Oh, when the   saints   go march- ing   in,

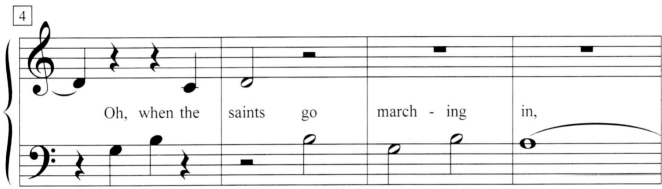

Oh,   when the   saints   go   march - ing   in,

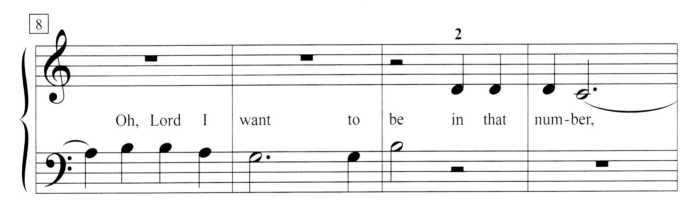

Oh,   Lord   I   want   to   be   in   that   num-ber,

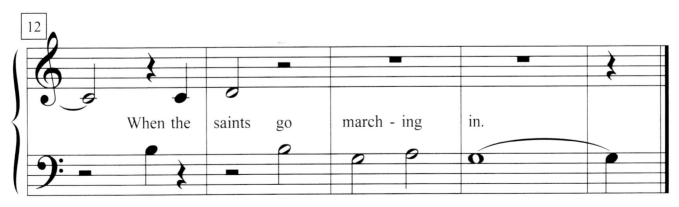

When the   saints   go   march - ing   in.

Jazzy Fingers

Words by Wesley Schaum

Adapted from Betsy Barrett

Duet Accompaniment

 Track 3: Performance tempo
Track 4: Practice tempo (played twice)

Birds Rock

Words by Wesley Schaum

John W. Schaum

Moderato

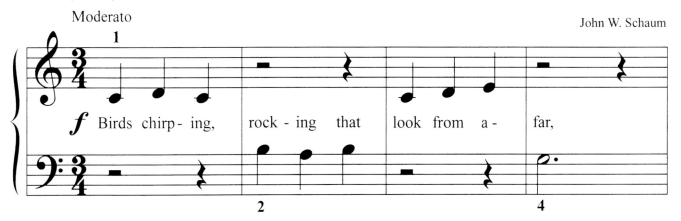

Birds chirp - ing, rock - ing that look from a - far,

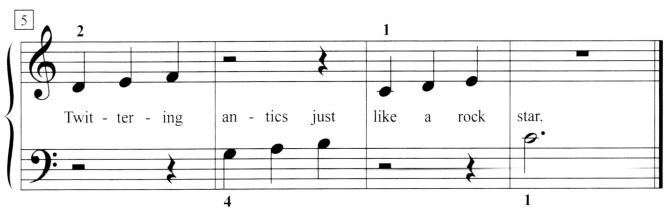

Twit - ter - ing an - tics just like a rock star.

Duet Accompaniment

Track 5: Performance tempo
Track 6: Practice tempo (played twice)

Twinkle, Twinkle Little Star

Words by Jane Taylor

French folk tune

Twin - kle, twin - kle, lit - tle star, How I won - der

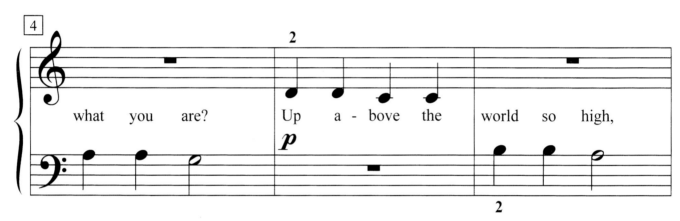

what you are? Up a - bove the world so high,

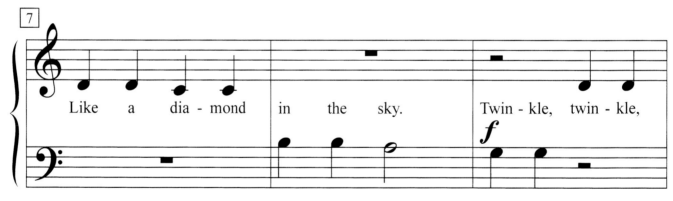

Like a dia - mond in the sky. Twin - kle, twin - kle,

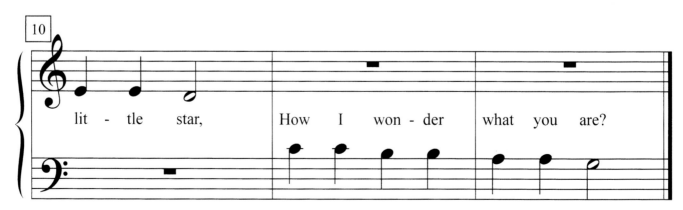

lit - tle star, How I won - der what you are?

This piece uses music from France and words from England. The music originated in France in the middle 1700's. In 1785, Mozart used it for a set of theme and variations. The words for *Twinkle, Twinkle Little Star* are part of a group of English poems by Jane Taylor, written in the early 1800's. The words and music were put together in 1881. The same music is also used for the familiar Alphabet Tune: *A, B, C, D, E, F, G.*

Duet Accompaniment: *Play One Octave Higher Throughout*

Track 7: Performance tempo
Track 8: Practice tempo (played twice)

When boogie music originated in the United States during the 1930's, it was called *boogie woogie*. This style of piano music has roots in ragtime and jazz. There is usually a distinct re-petitive pattern in the bass. Some of the patterns are quite complicated and difficult to play. The duet part of this piece uses one pattern in measures 1-2 and 9-10. Another boogie pattern is found in measures 5-6 and 13-14.

Duet Accompaniment

 Track 9: Performance tempo
Track 10: Practice tempo (played twice)

Bubble Gum Boogie

Words by Wesley Schaum

Adapted from Alice M. McCullen

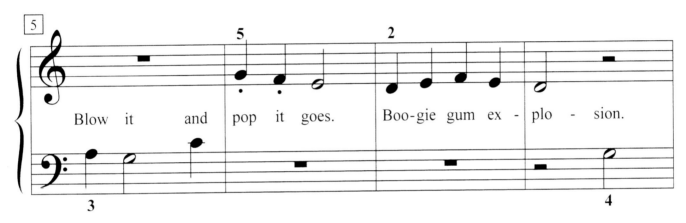

The source of the music for *Yankee Doodle* is unclear, but is probably from England in the middle 1700's. During that time there were many different poems which used this tune. The words for *Yankee Doodle* were first published in New York City as part of an American comic opera in 1767. *Yankee Doodle* was sung by American soldiers during the Revolutionary War (1775-1783) and has been very popular ever since.

Duet Accompaniment

 Track 11: Performance tempo
Track 12: Practice tempo (played twice)

Yankee Doodle

Vivace

Traditional American

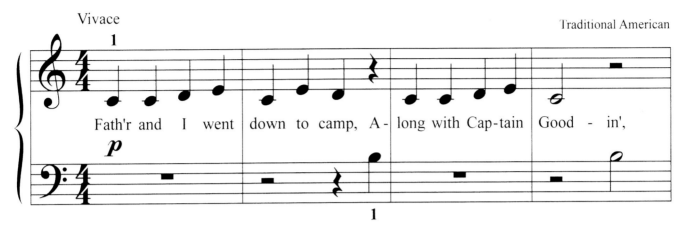

Fath'r and I went down to camp, A-long with Cap-tain Good - in',

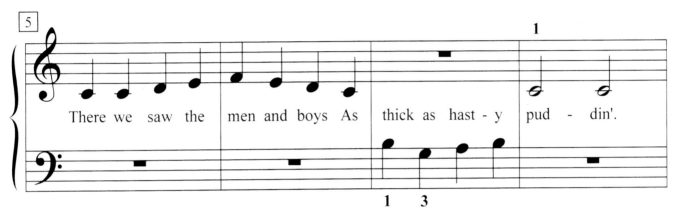

There we saw the men and boys As thick as hast - y pud - din'.

Yan - kee Doo - dle keep it up, Yan - kee Doo-dle dan - dy,

Mind the mu - sic and the step, And with the girls be hand - y.

Teacher's Note: The dotted quarter rhythm may be taught by rote, if desired.

America is one of our country's most beloved patriotic songs. It was first performed at a children's program in 1831 in Boston, Massachusetts with words written by Samuel Francis Smith. The origin of the music is uncertain, but is generally credited to Henry Carey in the middle 1700's. The music has been used ever since for the English national anthem, "God Save the Queen" or "God Save the King," depending upon who is the monarch. In 1804, Beethoven wrote a set of theme and variations using this music.

Duet Accompaniment

 Track 13: Performance tempo
Track 14: Practice tempo (played twice)

America

Words by Samuel F. Smith

M. Henry Carey

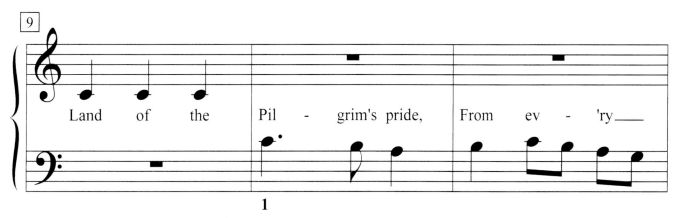

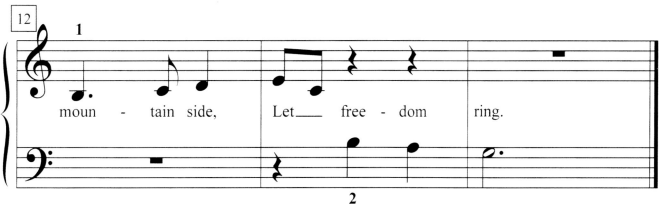

14

This famous wedding march, often known as "Here Comes the Bride," is by the German opera composer, Richard Wagner (1813-1883). His name is pronounced *VAHG-ner*. An opera is a musical drama with lots of singing and an orchestral accompaniment. Wagner's operas are lengthy theater productions with elaborate scenery, costumes, lighting and special effects. This music is used for a wedding scene in his opera, *Lohengrin*. Wagner wrote 12 other operas, many of which are still performed in large cities in the United States and Europe.

Duet Accompaniment

 Track 15: Performance tempo
Track 16: Practice tempo (played twice)

Wedding March

Adagio

Richard Wagner

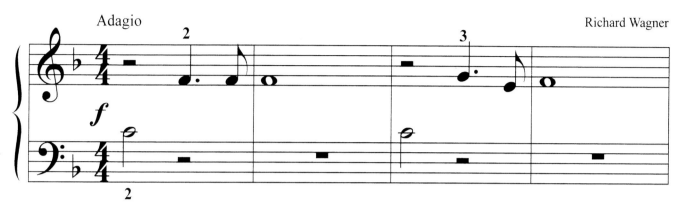

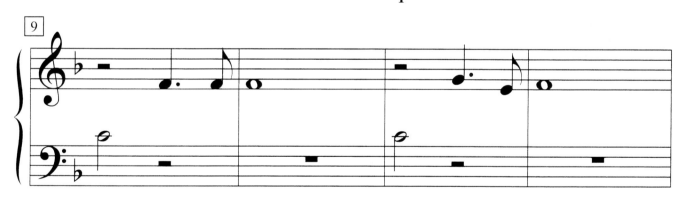

Rock music often uses patterns of repeated notes in groups of three. The duet part for this piece uses these patterns as an accompaniment.

Rock music started in the United States in the 1950's when it was called "Rock 'n' Roll." It became very popular in many parts of the world. There is now a Rock 'n' Roll Museum in Cleveland, Ohio. Glitzy costumes, fancy guitars, concert posters and sheet music of famous rock performers are included in the displays.

Duet Accompaniment

 Track 17: Performance tempo
Track 18: Practice tempo (played twice)

Rocking Penguins

Moderato

Words and music by Wesley Schaum

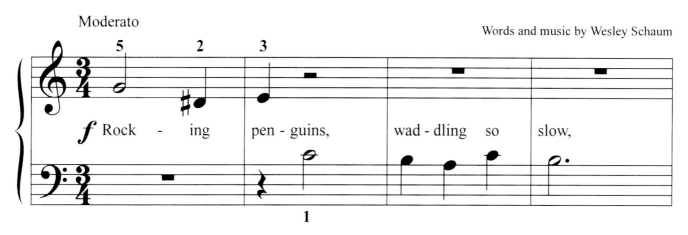

f Rock - ing pen - guins, wad - dling so slow,

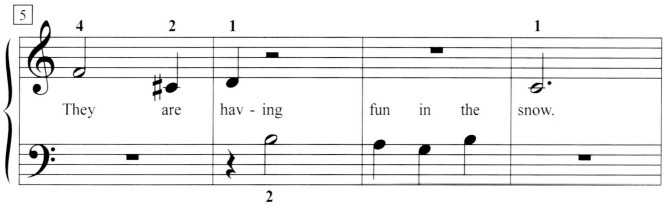

They are hav - ing fun in the snow.

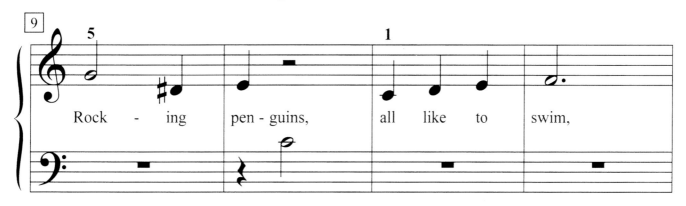

Rock - ing pen - guins, all like to swim,

They are pad - dling through thick and thin.

The *can-can* is a vigorous high-kicking dance that was very popular in cabarets and dance halls during the 1860's in Paris, France. At that time, it was considered naughty and daring because women flounced their skirts revealing their well-covered legs. The composer, Jacques Offenbach (1819-1880) is most famous for over 97 comic operas written during his lifetime.

Duet Accompaniment

 Track 19: Performance tempo
Track 20: Practice tempo (played twice)

Can Can

Animato

Jacques Offenbach

20

The words to *America the Beautiful* were written as a poem in 1895 by Katherine Lee Bates. It is said that she was inspired by a visit to the top of Pikes Peak, Colorado which has a spectacular view of the surrounding landscape. Her words were later combined with a hymn tune written by Samuel A. Ward. This combination of words and music was so popular that during the 1920's it was among the choices nominated to become our official national anthem.

Duet Accompaniment

 Track 21: Performance tempo
Track 22: Practice tempo (played twice)

America the Beautiful

Words by Katherine Lee Bates

Samuel Augustus Ward

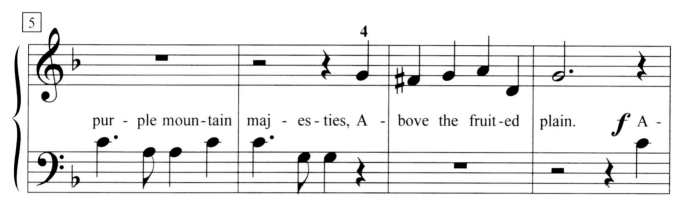

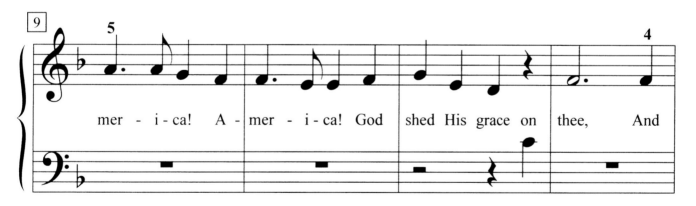

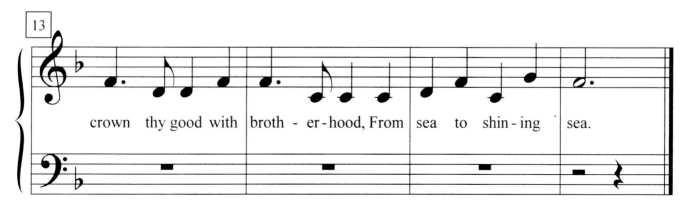

William Tell March

Allegro

Gioachino Rossini

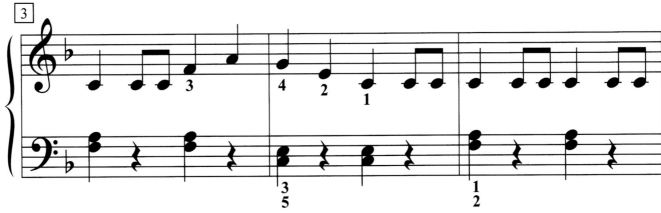

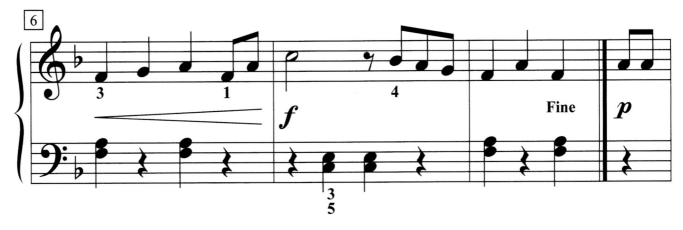

Duet Accompaniment

 Track 23: Performance tempo
Track 24: Practice tempo (played twice)

This march from Rossini's opera *William Tell* is probably his most popular theme. The rhythm, which resembles the hoofbeats of a horse, has been used as background music in countless cartoon shows in movies and TV. Rossini (row-ZEE-nee) is one of Italy's most famous opera composers. He wrote his first opera at age 14. By age 18 he had also written two symphonies. During his lifetime he wrote 40 operas, of which *William Tell* is the last.

Duet Accompaniment – *continued*

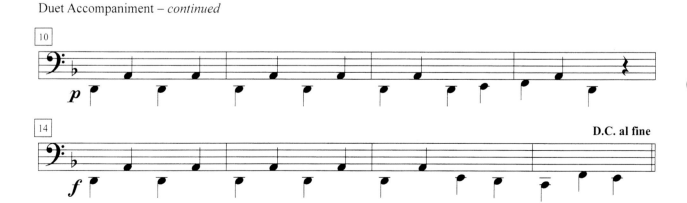

MORE GREAT SCHAUM PUBLICATIONS

FINGERPOWER®

by John W. Schaum

Physical training and discipline are needed for both athletics and keyboard playing. Keyboard muscle conditioning is called technic. Technic exercises are as important to the keyboard player as workouts and calisthenics are to the athlete. Schaum's *Fingerpower*® books are dedicated to development of individual finger strength and dexterity in both hands.

00645334	Primer Level – Book Only	$6.99
00645016	Primer Level – Book/Audio	$8.99
00645335	Level 1 – Book Only	$6.99
00645019	Level 1 – Book/Audio	$7.99
00645336	Level 2 – Book Only	$6.99
00645022	Level 2 – Book/Audio	$7.99
00645337	Level 3 – Book Only	$6.95
00645025	Level 3 – Book/Audio	$7.99
00645338	Level 4 – Book Only	$6.99
00645028	Level 4 – Book/Audio	$8.99
00645339	Level 5 Book Only	$6.99
00645340	Level 6 Book Only	$6.99

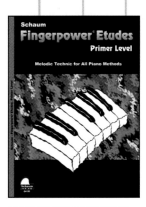

FINGERPOWER® ETUDES

Melodic exercises crafted by master technic composers. Modified or transposed etudes provide equal hand development with a planned variety of technical styles, key, and time signatures.

00645392	Primer Level	$6.95
00645393	Level 1	$6.99
00645394	Level 2	$6.99
00645395	Level 3	$6.95
00645396	Level 4	$6.99

FINGERPOWER® FUN

arr. Wesley Schaum
Early Elementary Level

Musical experiences beyond the traditional *Fingerpower*® books that include fun to play pieces with finger exercises and duet accompaniments. Short technic prepartory drills (finger workouts) focus on melodic patterns found in each piece.

00645126	Primer Level	$6.95
00645127	Level 1	$6.95
00645128	Level 2	$6.95
00645129	Level 3	$6.95
00645144	Level 4	$6.95

FINGERPOWER POP

Arranged by James Poteat

10 great pop piano solo arrangements with fun technical warm-ups that complement the Fingerpower series! Can also be used as motivating supplements to any method and in any learning situation.

00237508	Primer Level	$9.99
00237510	Level 1	$9.99
00282865	Level 2	$9.99

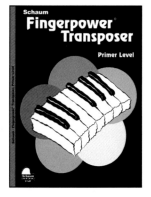

FINGERPOWER® TRANSPOSER

by Wesley Schaum
Early Elementary Level

This book includes 21 short, 8-measure exercises using 5-finger patterns. Positions are based on C,F, and G major and no key signatures are used. Patterns involve intervals of 3rds, 4ths, and 5ths up and down and are transposed from C to F and F to C, C to G and G to C, G to F and F to G.

00645150	Primer Level	$6.95
00645151	Level 1	$6.95
00645152	Level 2	$6.95
00645154	Level 3	$6.95
00645156	Level 4	$6.95

JUMBO STAFF MANUSCRIPT BOOK

This pad features 24 pages with 4 staves per page.

00645936		$4.25

CERTIFICATE OF MUSICAL ACHIEVEMENT

Reward your students for their hard work with these official 8x10 inch certificates that you can customize. 12 per package.

00645938		$6.99

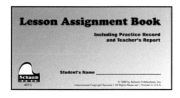

SCHAUM LESSON ASSIGNMENT BOOK

by John Schaum

With space for 32 weeks, this book will help keep students on the right track for their practice time.

00645935		$3.95

www.halleonard.com

Prices, contents, and availability subject to change without notice.